A Solemn Vow Of
SELF-C ELIBACY

A Commitment to Never Screw Yourself Again

Berwick Mahdi Davenport

A Solemn Vow of Celibacy
© Copyright 2020 Berwick Mahdi Davenport

All rights reserved. No part of this book may be used or reproduced in any manner whatsoever without written permission except in the case of brief quotations embodied in critical articles or reviews.

Brand It Beautifully™ Book Designs & Publishing
www.branditbeautifully.com

Edited by Janice Bradley, Editor of Exact Writing Services, LLC

Printed in the United States of America

TABLE OF CONTENTS

Introduction 1
Mixed Messages 4
Let's Get Back To Us 9
Trina's Deep Dark Secret 13
The 27 Confessions 22
Am I About To Screw Myself? 28
Tripping Myself...32
How It Happens 35
The Truth You Should Never Sacrifice 40
The Truth About Being Authentic............................42
The Side Effects..45
There's A Lot We Don't Know 49
It's All About Ego 52
Soul-Focused Or Worldy-Focused 57
An Ego That Mirrors Your Soul...............................63
Possession Is 9/1O Of The Law 65
Hypnotize Your Ego 71
Adam's First Job..75
At The Center 77
Signs And Signals...82
The Vow 87

This Book Contains Adult Language

Sometimes, if you're being true to what you're feeling, the most appropriate language to use can be viewed by others as inappropriate. It's the language we frown upon when spoken by others out in public. In fact, we pride ourselves on being able to say, "I never use language like that". It gives us a sense of self-righteousness. The truth is, people have been socialized to fear using certain words. It's because the mere utterance represents rebellion. Something inside that you've been suppressing is seeking to be released. The fact is, sometimes, no other language empowers us to release that energy except the expression of those taboo words.

Every culture has taboo language. However, when applied in the proper context, certain words have the power to release pent-up emotional energy resulting from past trauma. One of the first to stumble upon this was Sigmund Freud. He intentionally applied taboo language in his clinical practice in a therapeutic context to facilitate transformation.

"A Solemn Vow of Self-Celibacy" will, at times, deliberately use taboo language to achieve the same objective.

Introduction

There's a butterfly in your brain, waiting to come forth from the cocoon of your fears. The butterfly is your Eunoia. Eunoia is your beautiful, thinking mind. When what you're being or seeking to become in this world is in alignment with who you are, the butterfly in your brain comes forth.

A Solemn Vow of Self-Celibacy is the first step towards releasing your Eunoia. The vow to never screw yourself again is a part of the alignment process. To open the door to new never seen before possibilities, you need to create a spiritual clearing. Taking the vow is how you make room for a new level of happiness, health, and harmony. A Solemn Vow of Self-Celibacy is the single most radical act you can take to give yourself all that you desire. The wisdom in this vow is ancient. There is magic in it. When you take the vow, you release it into your life.

The wishes and desires of the conscious mind aren't necessarily the subconscious mind's wishes and desires. Often, they are in opposition to one another. When they aren't aligned, the subconscious cancels out our conscious intentions. By vowing to practice self-celibacy, you send the right signal to your subconscious mind to get in alignment with your conscious desires. A whole new world of possibilities opens up right before your eyes.

I wrote a Solemn Vow of Self-Celibacy to generate awareness around the fact that we've made screwing over ourselves a pattern that we must immediately interrupt. In fact, fucking over ourselves is the single most perverted spiritual act one can commit, and yet we do it regularly.

No one has ever screwed over us more than we've screwed over ourselves! No one has ever disappointed us more than we've disappointed ourselves. And no one has ever denied us permission to pursue our greatest desires more than ourselves.

We speak disparagingly about ourselves to ourselves, and we misrepresent our truth to the world. We have become masters of getting in our way.

Now just for a second, imagine how beautiful it would be if you woke up tomorrow, and you were one hundred percent on your own side. Every thought you think supports and encourages you to be your best.

You go the extra mile for yourself just as you do for others. You accept compliments and praise from others without guilt or suspicion.

You accurately represent your truth to others with pride. You see and appreciate your genius and openly celebrate it—no longer are you ashamed of any aspect of who you are.

Now, doesn't that feel good?

I want you to experience what it feels like to be one hundred percent on your own side, while you are alive. To experience Heaven on earth is a reality available to all those who no longer practice the dark art of screwing themselves.

By reading this book, you commit to the most important vow of your life- that vow is NEVER to screw yourself again.

MIXED MESSAGES

There's an old presentation formula that says when you're addressing an audience you should always, tell them what you're going to tell them, then tell them a second time then, once more, tell them again. It's the power of three. It helps people to retain the central theme of the presentation. A book is no different. I have found this formula to be highly effective and there's no reason for me to break from what works. So, here's what I'm about to tell you.

I'm about to tell you that your life works as well as your communication works. Whatever is unfolding in your life, the current consistent conditions are all mirror reflections of the messages you keep conveying to others and yourself through your communication. Stop for a second and consider the validity in what I've just said. See the wisdom in it. Your life, your relationship patterns and your experiences are all saying something about the messages you've been giving to the universe.

The world runs on communication and so does your life. The best way to change whatever you don't like about your life is to focus on the messages you're broadcasting. Here are three things most people don't understand about their communication yet desperately need to.

1. The universe does not fill in the blanks for you. Whatever you are not clear about in your communication equals leave everything exactly as it already is.

2. The universe does not make any decisions for you. The Law of Freewill forbids it. That means, if you don't say precisely what you desire, it equals to, you'll accept anything. In the end, it all equates to everything staying exactly as it already is.

3. There is no separate pot of communication in your life. All the messages you broadcast go into one collective pot. This collective pot makes up your consistent communication.

Now, here's what that means. It means what you tell God in private on your knees is not treated as something separate from the messages you're giving off when you're gossiping and complaining to your girlfriends or homeboys. It's also not disconnected from what you say to people on the streets or in the workplace. All your communication is one communication. It goes into one messaging pot. In most cases, that spiritual container ends up being a giant pot of mixed messages that causes you to keep manifesting the opposite of what you desire. In other words, the reason your life doesn't work the way you'd like for it to work is because your communication isn't broadcasting what is equal to what you desire. Mixed messaging means **everything stays exactly as it already is**. That is what our mixed messaging unconsciously conveys over to the Universe or God.

Now, if you're honest with yourself, there are stubborn areas in your life where nothing that you do changes anything. These conditions remain untouched because instead of being focused on fixing your communication, you've been trying to fix yourself. Your attempt to fix yourself has equated to changing yourself, which gives off a huge mix message. There is nothing wrong with who you are. However, there is most definitely something wrong with your communication.

Your communication is not who you are! It is what you are now or what you are seeking to become! What you are doesn't have any real power in it. It's like an egg without a yoke inside of it. Who you are is the yoke inside of the egg? Think of who you are as your natural expression. It's the power of God inside of yourself! Your communication represents who you are! All of your real power is in who you are. Who you are will never change! It's what you are that changes. When what you are, accurately represents who you are, your communication is brought to life. Once your conversation is animated, you can say something, and as a result of saying it, something powerful happens. That's the power of God inside of yourself.

On the other hand, when you say something and nothing happens, it's because you didn't integrate who you are into what you are. That means, your communication needs spiritual adjustment, alignment. What you are is out of sync with who you are. There is a cognitive distance between the two, and this distance saps your communication of power. The words that come from your mouth need to be powered up.

The average person's communication lacks animation because we are socialized not to communicate rather than how to. It's because rather than receiving natural education, we received performative education instead.

Natural education prepares you to take advantage of who you are. It helps you to understand who you are and how to apply the power in it to get what you desire from within yourself. Performative education, on the other hand, prepares you to be used by other people. It teaches you to see and think of power as something outside of yourself, something you need to get from other people and, thus, perform. Essentially, performative education is where we all first learn how to fuck ourselves.

So, I'm going to tell you how a "Solemn Vow of Self-Celibacy" restores power immediately to your communication; I'm also going to reveal what zapped the strength from your conversation in the first place. You must understand what caused you to develop the habit of broadcasting mixed messages so that you won't fall for the same tricks. Every time you give off mixed signals, you screw yourself out of what you most desire to experience.

I invite you to join me in taking a solemn vow to never screw myself again! I can think of no greater spiritual perversion than screwing over yourself. It all ends now!

LET'S GET BACK TO US

We are the beginning and end of everything involving us.

All roads lead back to us.

Our fingerprints are on everything.

We will never be able to get away from us, no matter where we go.

Our mark is on everything.

Our problems start with us and must end with us, if they are to end at all. Even the solution is inside of us. All roads lead straight back to us.

The problem is, we've been paying more attention to the roads that lead us away from us than the ones that point straight back to us.

We all have something to contribute to make this world a better place. To discover what yours is, you only need to study the one book to which you can never close your eyes. That book is, You. You see that? It keeps coming right back to you.

You are the twenty-four hours a day, book; the every second, and every moment of the day, book. The you are with yourself all the time, no matter where you are or what you're doing, book. There's no place you can go to get away from the book that is you. Did you know that there's a secret in the book about you?

You know how we always say, "God works in mysterious ways"? Well, your natural expression is your mysterious way. It's the part of you that's unpredictable, spontaneous and serendipitous. That means, it's uncontrollable and therefore unstoppable. It's the untethered power of your well-mind. Your natural expression is what empowers you to see what no one else can see. It is your vision that is your gift.

Some people believe their talent is their gift, but it's not. There are millions of other people who share the same talent as you and yet, they do not have the same gift. The power to see what no one else can see in the talent except you is the blessing. We are all prophets with the power to prophesy something that no one else can and through this, we profit.

Our natural advantage comes from our authentic sight. It is for this very reason that the moment we alter, or suppress our authenticity, we become the kryptonite to our own superpowers. We fuck ourselves. Our superpower is our authenticity. It is the secret we all must discover from reading the book that is ourselves.

Now that you know that you are the book, how long do you think it should take you to uncover the secret to your natural expression in the book?

Did you see that? That trick that was played on you? You still don't know what trick I'm talking about, do you? It's a major side effect resulting from repeatedly screwing yourself. I'm talking about the trick where you're allowed to be with yourself 24 hours a day, and yet you still wake up thirty, forty, fifty or even sixty years later, not knowing who you are and why you're here.

Do you know who you are and why you're here? If the answer is, "Not really – I'm still trying to figure it out", then know this. The only reason you haven't uncovered the truth about yourself is because you have a deep dark secret. You've been habitually screwing yourself, broadcasting mixed messages to the Universe. That's what not practicing Self-Celibacy does. It distracts you from getting to know enough about the one person you can never get away from to accurately represent their truth. As a result, you give off mixed messages. You sound confused.

At the very root of it there's really only one reason why we develop the ugly habit of screwing ourselves. It's because we've lost our mind. I mean, we no longer have possession of our Ego and need desperately to fully recapture it so we can direct it to an end of our own choosing. In other words, our Ego should be working for us, not the world. To achieve this endeavor, you'll need to understand what caused you to lose your mind, in the first place. What is our Ego's kryptonite?

Taking a Solemn Vow of Self-Celibacy is the quickest, most effective way to take possession of your Ego, redefine it and then direct it to an end of your Soul's choosing.

TRINA'S DEEP DARK SECRET

Trina only has twenty dollars left to her name and she's going to have to use it to get some food to feed herself and her five-year-old daughter, Jasmine. To top it off the power company has just turned off the electricity to her apartment. She hasn't paid her bill in two months. Fortunately, she had already dropped Jasmine off at school before the power was turned off.

There's Trina, sitting in what would be total darkness if it weren't for the fact that it's daylight outside. The fact that it's summer, means soon it's going to be too hot to bear in her apartment. She doesn't have a clue as to what she's going to do. Trina was recently laid off from her job at the local grocery store and she doesn't have anyone else to call on. She's been on her own for a while now. So, there she is, sitting on the edge of her bed crying, afraid of what's going to happen next. Out of a humble act of desperation Trina drops to her knees and starts praying, just as she remembered her grandmother telling her to do. She could hear her voice saying to her, "God answers prayers".

In that moment, Trina comes clean. She confesses to God her wrongs, silly mistakes and her reoccurring hardheaded decisions. After confessing, she begs God to show her the way out of her condition. She promises to do whatever God tells her to do. "I'm ready to make that change, Lord," are her exact words.

I want you to know that Trina did not get to where she is by accident. She's had lots of opportunities, but like so many others, she too was hellbent on screwing herself. In all honesty, she's become quite good at it. It doesn't take her long to fuck herself over and then blame other people. She's been misrepresenting her truth for as far back as she can remember. Her Ego fell victim to kryptonite when she was just a little girl.

Before this moment there was nothing anyone else could say to her that would stop her from screwing herself. Hiding from people in plain sight was what she did best. She hid in her communication. That means, she broadcasted messages to people that misrepresented the truth of life. No one knows Trina's accurate location. Perhaps, this moment will turn out to be different. Sometimes hitting rock bottom has a way of killing your Ego, so you can give birth to a new one; an Ego that mirrors your Soul. As my grandmother would often say, "A hard head makes for a soft ass."

To make a long story short, Trina dries her tears, gets off her knees and heads out to the local grocery store where she used to work. She's going to use her last twenty dollars to buy a few things to eat. She selects her items from the shelf and then makes her way to the cash register. As she's approaching the cashier, she sees her friend, Tia, from high school.

Trina and Tia were besties. They did everything together, but secretly there was rivalry. Trina privately competed with her and whenever possible would always try to outdo Tia. So, there is Tia standing at the register looking like a million bucks. She's sporting one of those power suits women sometimes wear when you know they're about to handle some major business. Trina sees Tia, but Tia doesn't see her. Immediately, Trina ducks off, and swiftly heads back down the aisle, towards the back of the store.

She's thinking to herself, "The last thing I need is for that heffa to see me looking like this. If she does, everyone is going to know my business." So, she stalls for time, walking up and down one aisle after another until she believes Tia has already left the store.

Would you like to know why Trina doesn't want Tia to see her like this? I mean, besides the fact that they used to be rivals, and Trina is looking tore up to the floor up.

It has something to do with the fact that when they graduated from high school, they both had plans to become lawyers. Tia went off to college, but Trina stayed. She told Tia she wanted to have one more year of fun before she went off to college. The truth was, her grades weren't good enough, but she never wanted Tia to know. Fast forward ten years later and Trina is in the condition she is right now, while Tia is now a highly successful partner in her own law firm. Trina doesn't know any of this, because they haven't spoken to one another in ten years.

Okay back to Trina ducking off between the aisles in the grocery store, to avoid being seen by her girlfriend, Tia. By now, she figures that Tia has left the building so she makes her way back to the cashier to pay for her groceries. She reaches into her pocket to retrieve the twenty-dollar bill and it falls to the floor. As she reaches down to pick it up, she looks up and guess who's standing right there behind her? Yep, you guessed it; Tia. Trina raises up and Tia gives her a great big warm hug. You can tell it was genuine. Tia sincerely missed her girlfriend. On top of that you could tell that Tia has been working on herself. No longer is she the insecure teenager she once was. She knows who she is and embraces it. Tia has taken full possession of her mind. Her Ego is working for her and not against her.

"Hey girl, it's so wonderful to see you", is what Tia voices to Trina. Trina returns the expression. "Tell me. How have you been doing, Tia?" asked Trina. Tia starts to tell her all about the things she's accomplished and the success she's been having in her law practice. "Enough about me Trina. Tell me what's going on with you, girlfriend." A silent pause fills the air. It's that moment of truth that in which we sometimes find ourselves when what we say to God in private is now being put to the test in public. Remember what Trina promised, God? She asked for a way out. Little does she know that this may very well be that door. Here's her chance to take a firm step towards becoming self-celibate. All she has to do is be honest and resist her tendency to screw herself.

Okay, stop for a second. Before I tell you the rest of the story, I want you to tell me what you think Trina is going to say to Tia. Do you think Trina is going to be honest or will she make something up in an attempt to make herself look good in Tia's eyes?

If you guessed that she would make something up, then you're correct. Trina tells Tia that everything is going great, couldn't be better. Imagine that! All those painful tears she cried on her knees in her dark apartment and just that quick, she's fucking herself again. Wow! You talk about some perverted-ass shit. One of the most difficult things to watch is someone screwing themselves.

Trina even goes as far as to makes up some story about how she's just started her own business and is making lots of money and meeting successful people. Damn! She did that!

Tia congratulates her and gives her another warm hug. They exchange numbers and Tia walks out of the store towards her car. As Trina is standing there paying for her items, she begins to reflect on what she's just done. She just broadcasted a major mixed message. That's right, Trina just fucked herself and she really doesn't have an idea to what extent. This time something different happens. She remembers what she promised God while on her knees. She jumps into action and in an attempt to rectify her mistake she jets out to the parking lot to stop Tia from leaving. Tia gets out of her car and Trina does something truly amazing. She confesses to Tia that she lied. Wow! She doesn't realize it, but she's taking a huge step towards becoming self-celibate.

She comes clean right in the face of her long-time high school rival. Now that's some powerful shit. In one swoop Trina frees herself from the mental prisons in which she's been secretly doing time right in people's faces. She no longer has to be ashamed or afraid of her own truth. Liberating. With tears rolling down her cheeks she sobs in shame from just the thought of what she almost did to herself once again. Tia hugs her tight and then reassured her that everything is going to be alright.

Then Tia starts to explain the real reason why she had come to town. "Girl, you're not going to believe this, but I came to town looking for you. I just purchased a huge high-rise apartment complex and I needed someone to help manage it for me. The only person I could think of was you. I know we haven't spoken in years, but I know I can trust you. The thing is, when you said you had started your own business I didn't want to interfere with your success and so I didn't say anything". Trina's mouth dropped. She can't believe what she's just heard her girlfriend say. Overwhelmed by the joy that follows redemption, she shouts the words, "Thank you, thank you, thank you – Lord thank you," is all she could say.

Hopefully, you get the picture. Trina, just like so many others in a similar situation was about to fuck herself for the exact same reason as all the rest of us. We are ashamed of the current state of our reality and so, we misrepresent our truth to others to hide it. We are dishonest. That means, we don't tell the truth that we struggle to tell, to the people we struggle most to tell it to. In other words, we lack the courage to face our own fears. What we don't realize is that each time we fail to accurately represent our own truth we screw ourselves out of all sorts of opportunities. We block our own blessings. That's what screwing yourself does to you. It blocks your blessing. Taking a Solemn Vow of Self-Celibacy opens the door to heaven on earth.

Are you ready to stop blocking your fortune? Have you fucked yourself over enough to realize that as long as you continue to do this to yourself you cannot win? If you are, then at the end of my book you will be asked to enter into a spiritual contract. You will be invited to take a Solemn Vow of Self-Celibacy. Taking it means you're confessing to having screwed yourself repeatedly and then promising God to never fuck yourself again, under the penalty of death.

Did you feel that? I'm talking about that feeling you got in the pit of your stomach when you heard me say, under the penalty of death. That's what real spiritual accountability feels like. In other words, there is no reason for any of us to have the earth suit we're in, if all we're going to do is sit around and fuck ourselves. I'm pretty sure, there are other spirit beings who would love to have that suit you're in right now. It's time to power up your communication so you can power up your life.

Just in case you're still having problems figuring out what Self-Celibacy means then listen to this. Self-Celibacy means you are no longer committing the perverted act of screwing yourself. Your communication is one hundred percent on your own side. Nothing that comes from your mouth goes against what you desire for yourself. It also means that no one can get you to stand against yourself again. You are committing yourself to being your best friend.

Being one hundred percent on your own side looks like not finding something wrong with who you naturally are. It's your "Yes's" being "Yes" and your "No's" being, "No". You have no more fake yes's or no's to handout. You shut down your bullshit factory. That means, no more throwing pity parties for yourself, making excuses, blaming other people or telling disempowering stories about why you haven't been able to succeed. You finally realize that there is nothing you can think, say or do that can take you off the hook for being responsible for the life you desire to live.

If you choose not to take a Solemn Vow of Self-Celibacy, there will be no judgement or love lost. In other words, no one will make fun of you or ridicule you. Not everyone who reads my book is ready to stop fucking themselves. There will be some who will need to dig a deeper hole for themselves before they realize just how spiritually perverted the act of screwing themselves is. The thing is, after reading this book you will never be able to say you didn't know what screwing yourself does to you! That said, I have something I want to confess. Here it is: the only reason why I know so much about what screwing ourselves is like is because I used to fuck over myself on a regular basis. I became a master at it and here's what I discovered as a result.

THE 27 CONFESSIONS

Screwing yourself always leaves evidence, forensics. Our mixed messaging snitches on itself. It doesn't matter if we confess to doing it ourselves or not, because the evidence it leaves behind always does. Evidence is a confession in and of itself. You can say you're not fucking yourself all you like, and it might sound convincing to those who don't know what to look for. However, as soon as you discover how to read the signs, the forensics speak for themselves. The reason I'm able to provide such a detailed list of evidence is because these were all the ways that I screwed myself. These are my original 27 Confessions.

I'm not attempting to shame you or make you feel guilty. To the contrary, I'm offering you the opportunity to get naked before you have to stand naked. When I say, get naked I'm not taking about taking off all your clothes. You see, you can take off all your clothes, and yet still not be naked at all. Today, people have very little concern about taking off their clothing; what they struggle with however, is getting naked, being transparent and authentic in their expression.

Naked was Adam and Eve's original state of being. They were naked. They had nothing to hide. They lived transparent lives. That was until they started screwing themselves. They fucked themselves right out of the garden of Eden. And the first piece of evidence that told on them came from the fact that they were hiding in the bushes from God. They were broadcasting mixed messages directly in God's face. Oh, by the way, we are always directly in God's face. Remember, all our communication goes into one pot. Besides, God knows the truth even before you speak it, lie about it or try to hide it like Adam and Eve did in the story.

There is no place to hide from God. Only if you're screwing yourself would you ever believe there is some place to hide from God. To think that they could hide was evidence that they had bitten off of the real forbidden fruit. I call it the true lies. Essentially, the serpent turned them on to fucking themselves while simultaneously turning them off to God. I know you want to blame everything on Adam and Eve, after all that's what we've been taught to believe. However, here's what you need to understand.

Adam and Eve had never come into contact with a lie ever before in their entire lives. And so, they had no way of defending themselves against it. They didn't even know that they should defend themselves. They were innocent like children. So, they accepted what the serpent told them as the truth. Lying was a new technology, and the serpent laced it kryptonite. First, he told them who they were, which was not who God had created them to be. This gave birth to an Ego not Mated with their Soul. He told them they weren't like God, which was a lie. Remember, as the story goes God created them in his own image and likeness. That means they were already just like God. To sweeten the pot, the serpent threatened them with the possibility of not being good enough, rejection. That is Ego kryptonite. So, in Adam and Eve's attempt to fix themselves, they hid themselves from God, their creator.

Without even saying it, their attempt to fix themselves broadcasted the message that God had made a mistake. That was why Adam and Eve hid. They thought they weren't good enough, not realizing that if they weren't then their Creator must have also not been good enough. That's the mixed messages you keep broadcasting to the universe.

The evidence that you're trying to fix yourself always speaks for itself. Evidence is the silent confession you make without even knowing that you're making it. Here are my original 27 confessions.

The 27 Confessions

As long as…

1. You're comparing yourself to other people.

2. You're exaggerating to impress people.

3. There are people whose approval you're trying to win.

4. There are people with whom you're competing.

5. You're not honest.

6. You're still bullshitting.

7. You can describe what you don't want in more detail than what you do want.

8. You believe you're not good enough.

9. You don't completely trust yourself.

10. The thoughts you think aren't a hundred percent on your own side.

11. You still haven't figured out how to capitalize on your genius.

12. You're unable to sustain your authenticity from one relationship to another.

13. You're unable to share the spotlight with others without causing conflict.

14. What other people think about you is more important than what you think about yourself.

15. Being right is more important than getting what you want.

16. Looking good is more important than feeling good.

17. You're forcing yourself to do what you don't want to do.

18. Your yes's aren't real yes's and your no's aren't real no's.

19. You're not demonstrating respect for your own experiences.

20. You can see why you're going to fail but not how you're going to succeed.

21. Your negative experiences are someone else's fault.

22. You keep doing the same thing over and over again and expecting different results.

23. You're pretending to be something you're not.

24. You're attempting to live up to someone else's definition of you.

25. You want other people to listen to you, but you don't listen to yourself.

26. You're not translating what things mean to you to other people.

27. You're not giving your accurate location.

The appearance of any of the 27 Confessions tells us that even on an unconscious level we're broadcasting mixed messages. In short, we're screwing ourselves. Once you take a solemn vow of self-celibacy, an indelible question will come to life within both your conscious and subconscious mind. "Am I about to fuck myself?" is the question.

Am I About to Screw Myself?

Would you like to know exactly where screwing yourself takes you? It takes you straight to mental prison, where you are allowed to look at your desires, but never get to fully experience them. There's nothing like it. When you screw yourself, it sentences you to your very own, tailor made, mobile prison for your mind. In other words, the side effects of not taking a solemn vow of self-celibacy is living your life inside your head. That's the prison.

There, your thoughts run incessantly, and you're left with worrying about what could happen if you lose. You take inventory of it in your mind and can clearly articulate it to others. In other words, your mind remains more focused on the negative possibilities, rather than the positive ones. You're consumed by false evidence appearing real, so much so, until you don't even notice just how much you're habitually fucking yourself; not completely on the side of your own desires.

I know what it's like because I've been there. I've done hard time in my own mental prison, unconsciously consumed by the virtual fears of my Ego. All I could think of was how I would look to other people if I allowed myself to go all out after what I desired and failed. What would people think of me? I found it safer to pretend that I was all in rather actually going all in. I rationalized to myself that if I lost, then at least I had mitigated the pain associated with losing.

What I didn't realize was that I was betraying myself. I began to understand why I had no problem going all out to help someone else get what they wanted out of life, yet I wouldn't go all out for my own desires. It was because screwing myself had become my addiction. It was such a secret that even I didn't know that I was doing it to myself. In fact, if you had asked me back then I would have sworn on a stack of Bibles that someone else was screwing me over, not me. The last thing I wanted to admit to myself was that it was me the entire time.

The fact that I wasn't totally on my own side meant I frequently hauled my body into spaces where I wasn't fully present. We do it all the time, not realizing that each time we do it we're cheating ourselves out of something that we can only receive as a result of being fully present. As soon as I would sit my black ass down in the chair my mind would swiftly leave my body to time travel into either the future or the past. So, technically speaking, I was physically present, but mentally and spiritually I was absent, at the same time. That's a mixed message.

Each time we show up physically present but consciously absent, we create an incomplete experience. An incomplete experience is a mixed message. Consider how often you drag your body into places and then withdraw your consciousness from your body while you travel in your mind and attend to other matters. You think nothing of it because it's normal for you to do it. In fact, it's normal to you and yet it's not natural. There is a huge difference! Being one hundred percent on your own side is natural. We are born this way. Not being totally on your own side is unnatural, yet in this world we've made it normal. We multitask our life away. That means we spend a great deal of our time in split consciousness, failing to be fully present anywhere.

Essentially, it means your awareness is not all the way in your body. When this happens it's impossible to experience the fullness of the moment. Each time I sent mixed messages all I could manage to do was rack up one incomplete experience after another. Incomplete, incomplete and incomplete. That's what my life mirrored back to me.

When you rack up more incompletes than completes, regrets start to pile up. With those regrets come resentment, guilt and shame. You want to be present, but you can't seem to find the right amount of incentive to stay focused. And so, when you're supposed to be present, you end up traveling to someplace else inside your mind. How can anyone be fully present when a part of their mind is trapped in multiple incomplete experiences?

It is for this reason when you're locked behind mental bars nothing makes you happy. You can be a billionaire, with your own private island, have servants waiting on you hand and foot, and yet you're still going to be miserable. It's because you no longer have the power to be present. Your thoughts are always focused on something else. No one can enjoy their life as long as their mind is serving two opposite wills. Mental servitude is the side effect that comes along with broadcasting mixed messages. It's like wanting to be in love, yet at the same time telling other people that you're not ready for love. It's a mixed message you're giving to yourself and the universe, and what it's doing is putting you in your own way.

Imagine someone running as fast as they can and then tripping themselves. If screwing yourself were a sport it would look like that. The objective of the game would be to see who can run the fastest and then trip themselves the hardest. The one that breaks their leg in the most areas wins. That's us fucking ourselves!

TRIPPING MYSELF

I remember when my ex-wife and I had first moved to Houston, Texas after escaping Hurricane Katrina. We moved into a small apartment type house and we swiftly outgrew it. We both wanted a bigger house, but in all honesty, I was afraid to lean all the way into my desire. Nevertheless, sometimes when I wasn't paying attention to my fears. I would allow myself to imagine what it would be like to get the home of my desires.

That said, there was the subdivision close to where we lived at the time that I frequently drove by just about every day. It was a beautiful gated community with huge waterfalls on both sides of the gate, stock ponds full of fish, and at night it would be lit up like a Christmas tree. I remember driving by that subdivision and whispering to myself, "Boy, I would sure like to live in there." That was a frequent occurrence. Almost at the same time that I imagined how nice it would be to live there, in the next breath inside my head I was telling myself that I couldn't afford it. Why even waste my time getting my hopes up? To make a long story short I treated that subdivision like a "someday" kind of dream, far off in the distance not requiring me to put any skin in the game.

One day while driving by the subdivision, I received a phone call from my ex-wife, Stephanie, asking me to meet her at a particular address. I didn't realize it at first, but the address she communicated to me was that same subdivision. Without realizing it I found myself driving through the same gated community that I was convinced we couldn't afford. In my mind, I was like, "Stephanie must have made a mistake. She knows we can't afford to live in here." I had already started to screw myself and I hadn't even looked at the house yet.

So, I get to the house, get out the car and Stephanie gets out of hers. Immediately, I walk up to her and start trying to get her to join me in screwing ourselves over. I say to Stephanie, "You know we can't afford this." She replies, "No, I don't know that. Let's just go in and see. You never know!" We walk into the house and we both instantly fall in love it. Nevertheless, I'm still whispering the same crap in Stephanie's ear. Fast forward, it turns out we were the only people interested in purchasing the home. We sat down to speak with the owners who were African. We asked them to tell us why they wanted to sell the house. They told us there was a grave family emergency back home in Africa to which they had to tend. They told us how much money they wanted for the house and just as I figured, we couldn't afford it. Well, at least that's what I thought.

When I expressed to them that we couldn't afford it, they responded, "Well then, what can you afford?" We told them what we could afford and then they accepted it, just like that. Turns out, it was exactly what we could afford, and it was exact place I had day-dreamed of living.

The moral of the story is that if it weren't for Stephanie, who was already practicing self-celibacy we would have missed out on a huge blessing. My mixed messaging would have screwed us out of the home we both wanted. Here's why: if it was left up to me alone, I wouldn't have leaned into my desire for the home enough to even cooperate with going to the open house. I was screwing myself far too much to lean into my desire.

I was living in conflict. If it weren't for Stephanie being fully committed to what she desired I would have screwed us out of it. I learned a lot from this experience. It compelled me to want to uncover the impetus behind how we develop the habit of screwing ourselves. Children aren't born screwing themselves. They lean into what they desire fully. They believe in the possibilities and are totally committed to what they want. The world socializes us to fuck ourselves and here's an example of how it starts.

HOW IT HAPPENS

It's early Monday morning at work. Jessica hasn't even had a chance to make herself comfortable at her desk before her boss is already calling her into his office. She can tell by the abrupt tone in his voice that he's upset about something. She's one of few people of color that work in the office, and he tends to take a more abrasive approach whenever he communicates with her. This time, apparently, the quarterly report Jessica submitted, had two errors on it. It wasn't much, but he's been looking for a reason to jam her up for a while.

Without giving it a second thought, he starts hurling one misogynistic, race-based, microaggression filled comment at her, after another. It's pathetic and so is he. Nevertheless, it's something Jessica has made herself quite comfortable with. It's her reoccurring reality.

His comments are belittling and demoralizing. He hurls his words at her as if they were daggers aimed to kill. You can tell he wants to make her feel small and insignificant. He gets off on it! There's a lot Jessica wants to say but as usual she elects instead to swallow her pride.

Pride in this context has nothing to do with her Ego. It's all about family. Jessica is concerned about what would happen to her family if she lost her job. That's all that's on her mind, surviving so she can keep food on her table.

So, much like other women of color who came before her, Jessica simply puts on a fake smile, and then repeatedly utters the words, "Yes sir, I'm sorry. Yes sir. It won't happen again." She then heads back to her desk. With each step she takes, she can literally feel herself shrinking because she's losing just a little bit more of herself. The job is a whole lot more expensive than what she initially thought it would cost.

There's a price we pay for everything, even working at a job that pays us money. What it's costing Jessica is far more expensive than the paper money she's receiving in return. Jessica is in between a rock and a hard place. This job is costing her things that money cannot buy or replace; her dignity and integrity. The disrespect she's experienced is astounding. The very atmosphere makes it difficult for her to breathe.

In Jessica's mind, which is where she tends to spend most of her time while she's at work, she sits there imagining different scenarios of what would happen if she let people at work know what she was thinking. As usual, she concludes that to say anything would mean losing her job. So, she remains silent. It's silent on the outside, but it definitely isn't silent on the inside where a war is being waged. Nevertheless, this is the choice Jessica elects to make, resigned to the idea that it's better to sacrifice her authentic voice than lose her job. Jessica is screwing herself and in her own private thought world, she believes she has the perfect reason for doing so.

What Jessica doesn't realize is the fact that because she spends so much time at work, fucking herself has become a habit. At work, you can always find Jessica standing over to the side somewhere, screwing herself. She's been doing this for so long that she does it right in people's faces. She'll belittle her intelligence or downplay the significance of her contribution. She does this to make everyone else at work feel comfortable in her presence. She literally tries to make herself as small as possible so no one at work will feel threatened by her. It's exhausting!

When Jessica first started screwing herself, she only did it at work. As I mentioned before, the fact that she spends so much of her time at work means that before too long screwing herself has become a habit, maybe even an addiction. Now, she's a master at it. She not only does it at work, she'll screw herself at church, in the grocery store, and even in the presence of her girlfriends. It's pathetic! She's terrified to lean into her own desires and her own aspirations. Subsequently, she also doesn't trust herself and so, she's always looking to get someone else to co-sign on her decisions. "Am I doing it right or saying it right?" are the two internal questions she repeatedly asks herself. For all intents and purposes, Jessica is locked behind mental bars. She's doing time, and like almost anyone locked behind bars if you ask her how she got there, she'd tell you some shit about her boss at work, "He got me all locked up inside my head."

Have you ever heard of the word, bullshit? Well, bullshit is real. In this case, it's anything we think, say or do that we believe somehow takes us off the hook for being responsible for our own desires. Bullshit sounds like always playing the victim, giving excuses, throwing pity parties for ourselves, gossiping and telling disempowering stories about why we can't succeed. It's called bullshit because in reality nothing can strip us of the responsibility we have for making ourselves happy. Our health, happiness and harmony are on us.

The same rule applies to Jessica. Her future is in her hands, and sometimes that will require her to make difficult decisions. But one thing is for certain and that is this: nothing different can transpire if she doesn't do anything different. The one card Jessica has yet to play is the solemn vow of self-celibacy card. I promise you that when Jessica learns how to play the card, she'll never come out on the short end of the stick ever again.

The thing is, we can't find out what happens to us when we play the card without actually playing the card. There is a whole new life waiting for us on the other side of taking the vow.

As soon as anyone of us take the vow, we wholeheartedly accept responsibility for manifesting the life we desire to live. The field of possibilities is wide open, but when we screw ourselves, we are left with getting more of what we already have.

Remember, mixed messaging equates to getting more of what you already got, all the while believing you're going to get something different. It's insanity. If we keep entering the same variables into the equation, then there is no way to get a different result.

THE TRUTH YOU SHOULD NEVER SACRIFICE

What do we become when we elect to sacrifice our own truth for something else? We may choose to sacrifice it out of fear of losing our job, our partnership with someone, spouse divorcing us, or losing friendship. It doesn't matter. When we compromise our integrity, we forfeit our ability to be, and express, our whole selves. Until we stand in solidarity with ourselves, we exist in a state of internal confusion. We can generate physical presence but not spiritual presence. Psychologists call it cognitive dissonance. It's thinking one way and feeling another way and the two never connect. It's like having two separate wills operating inside of you, both pulling in two different directions. It makes it difficult to be all there.

Have you ever heard someone use the phrase, "They're not all there?" On the streets, it means that person is not all there because he or she has lost their mind. Don't think about what this means in the traditional sense; instead apply a more contemporary perspective. Instead, think of losing your mind as losing sight of yourself. It's the side effect of screwing yourself. When we lose sight of ourselves, we forfeit the power to be all here, now. Makes sense doesn't it? The place where we're not showing up fully present is in our communication. In other words, as I mentioned at the beginning of the book, we're broadcasting mixed messages. Doing so, means one thing. We're not all there. We're split between the present, the past, or the future. We're also split between being who we already are or being who other people want us to be.

Presence is proof of power! Generating presence means being one hundred percent on our own side; all in. That's what it takes to get into the zone. We have to be all in. There can be no lukewarm effort. It's all in or nothing When you fill your communication with all in messages you cause things to move in your favor.

THE TRUTH ABOUT BEING AUTHENTIC

I know we'd like to believe that we fuck ourselves because we can't be our authentic selves in the presence of certain people, but here's the deal. No one knows when you're being authentic except you. People around you may think they know your usual way of being or your consistent mental attitude. However, no one knows when you're disclosing your accurate location except you. People don't automatically assume that you're suffering from imposture syndrome. People give you the benefit of the doubt. They believe you're being authentic. People really don't have all that time to sit around and try to figure out whether or not you're being real. That's why every time you play the chameleon, whether you admit to it or not, you're short-changing yourself. You're standing in your own way. You're fucking yourself. Performative expression is screwing your natural expression.

Here's what happens the moment Jessica decides to swallow her authentic expression to save her job. She has been spiritually violated and elects to walk out of her boss's office without accurately representing her truth. Even though the event is over, Jessica will find it difficult to generate presence throughout the rest of her day. She will continue being drawn back to that moment with her boss. In fact, she might even become trapped there for a while. Jessica is going to want to have that moment back so she could say what she really wanted to say. However, because she didn't accurately represent her truth in the moment, she'll have no choice but to wait until a similar opportunity with her boss presents itself again.

Secretly, Jessica feels like she's betrayed herself and, in all honesty, she has. It is for this reason, she incessantly rehashes what happened in her mind, play by play; frame by frame. Each time she plays it back she experiences a small burst of regret and disappointment inside herself. No matter what anyone else says to her to make her feel better, in her gut she feels like a coward. If she could time travel back to that moment she would in a heartbeat? The problem is, she can't.

When you're in mental prison there is no escaping the agony of your own self-betrayal without facing up to the reality of your own truth. You have to own it. There is nothing else for you to own but your truth. To free yourself from mental prison you have to speak your truth in the moment that calls it forth. That's a big part of what taking a solemn vow of self-celibacy equates to; accurately representing your authenticity.

Jessica will only be able to redeem herself through an act of pure demonstration. If another moment like the one with her boss presents itself again, she'll have to demonstrate that she's practicing self-celibacy. Until then, a piece of her mind will remain stuck in that moment. Not realizing this Jessica will do what she has grown accustomed to doing and that's screwing herself even more.

Here's how Jessica doubles down on screwing herself. She calls up one of her girlfriends and tells her an entirely different version of the same event with her boss. She creates her own Twilight Zone episode. Jessica lies, describing the event in the exact opposite manner that it unfolded. She tells her girlfriend that she actually said everything she wanted to say and more, to her boss, but of course she didn't. She paints a picture of herself that makes her look like a badass shero, but it's all make-believe.

Why is Jessica doing this to herself? It's because she's trying to break out of her mental prison.

The trouble is, she can lie to everyone else, but she can't lie to herself. Jessica knows the truth, and she knows that she's just betrayed her own truth. Now that she's lied to her girlfriend, she'll have to remember the lie she told. The more lies she tells, the more lies she has to remember. Nothing taxes our memory more than having to remember lies, something that is not real. Lies aren't natural. The truth is natural. That being the case, you don't have to think about the truth to tell it. You only need to accurately represent it.

THE SIDE EFFECTS

Lying is the forbidden fruit. A fruit by definition is the fleshy product of the tree that contains seeds within it that can be eaten as food. Using fruit as a metaphor, both the truth and the lie contain seeds within it. The truth provides nourishment and the lie doesn't. The lie is just filler; empty calories without any real nutrients. In other words, no lie you tell or believe can support your being happy and fulfilled. Only truth and honesty can provide that support. When we start to give off mixed messages in our communication it's always because we're either telling lies or what we believe in is a lie and we don't know it. Anything that causes conflict in your life has a lie somewhere in it. Harmony and peace are products of the truth.

Just as the seeds of any fruit only produce more of that same fruit, likewise, does the lie produce more lies. When you tell one lie, it begets another. In fact, no one lie can stand alone. It needs backup. Like maggots on a dead corpse that will soon transform into flies, lies multiply. And well-organized lies can be more powerful than disorganized truths.

As all four of my grandmothers would say to me, *"If you tell one lie, you better tell two. Tell one for your brother and one for you."* It was their way of saying, once you tell one lie, you're going to have to cover up that lie with another one. With each lie you tell the road to redemption becomes more difficult to travel, because to redeem yourself will require you to come clean. In other words, each time we tell a lie we leave some aspect of our authentic self behind and to recover it we have to confess.

I believe this is why people say, *"A brave person only dies once, but a coward person dies a thousand times."* When we feel like a coward, it's because we left a piece of ourselves behind. There's a certain kind of agony that comes with it. We end up making it worse by stacking more lies on top of it. This makes it more difficult for us to come clean and reveal the truth. Imagine how difficult it's going to be for Jessica to come clean with her girlfriend. To get herself back she'll have to tell her girlfriend the truth. She'll have to do this to recover her own sanity.

We've all done what Jessica did; lied to someone else about what happened to us when we failed to accurately represent our truth. We did it for the same reason as Jessica. We were trying to free our mind from the torment of that moment. We never feel good about ourselves when we betray our truth. When we don't fully and maturely express our reality in the moment it is called for, a piece of ourselves gets trapped.

Each time we hold back what we have to contribute to the moment we create an incomplete experience. Jessica's moment with her boss is an example of an incomplete experience. Incomplete experiences operate on a loop. They repeatedly attract to themselves like events. It's the universe's way of giving us another chance to redeem ourselves. Jessica is racking up a lot of incompletes. The more incomplete experience we rake up the more mixed messages we broadcast out to the world.

How many times have you left a piece of yourself behind? How many times have you attempted to alter your natural expression to fit into someone else's expectation of you? Well, each time you did, you screwed yourself.

That's what this world has trained our Egos to do - fuck ourselves; and we've become quite good at it. No one who screws themselves can be trusted and it is for that same reason the average person does not fully trust themselves.

So, why does this keep happening, not to us, but through us? There's really only one reason and it's in what I revealed earlier. We've lost our mind! We're not all there! The only way for anyone to lose their mind is by either trying to live up or down to someone else's definition of them. In other words, instead of us focusing on becoming all of who we already are, we're focusing on becoming what other people (the world) want us to be.

Losing our mind is another way of saying we've lost sight of our Soul in the attempt to please everyone else.

The moment we become *of the world* it is then the world takes possession of our mind.

Have you ever wondered why you demonstrate genius when it comes to helping others but struggle to show that same brilliance when it comes to yourself? Consider how many times you've watched yourself go the extra mile for your boss at work yet when it comes down to yourself you can't seem to muster up the energy. What about being a regular problem solver in everyone else's life but your own. You're literally drowning in your own problems. Finally, have you ever wondered why your office space at work is so neat and organized while, your home closely resembles a pig's pen? Can you see the mixed messages? Whatever you do for someone else you should be able to do for yourself. When you can apply your talents to help others make lots of money but are unable to apply them to generate money for yourself there's a real problem, Houston. Here's the problem. Your mind isn't working for you. It's working for the world.

THERE'S A LOT WE DON'T KNOW

There's a lot we don't know about the mind but we're ashamed to admit it. If the average person truly understood their mind no one would ever suffer. If the old adage, "As a man thinketh, so is he," is true then the only thing you need to succeed in this world is possession of your mind.

When I command my mind to do something, I don't accept any excuses. I tell it don't come back to me with problems; come back to me with solutions. I treat my mind likes it's the magic genie in the lamp, because it is.

That being said, here are the twelve things I know about the mind that you also need to know.

I know:

1. We all have two minds. We have a first mind and a second mind.

2. We were born with our first mind, our Soul. It's our divine mind. Our connection to the eternal.

3. Our second mind is the mind we develop after we're born. It's called our

Ego. Ego is our earthly-manifesting mind.

4. Our second mind is supposed to work for our first mind, not the other way around. Our earthly-manifesting mind should be a reflection of our divine mind so that as it is in heaven, so it is on earth. As above, so below!

5. Our second mind is supposed do exactly what we tell it to do, when we tell it to do it.

6. Our Ego can't do what we tell it to do, as long as we don't have full possession of it.

7. Our second mind and the thoughts that occupy it will religiously screw us unless we take ownership of it.

8. Our second mind is in charge of our communication and will broadcast mixed messages to the universe, as long as someone else is in possession of it.

9. We can only take possession of our second mind by taking a Solemn Vow of Self-Celibacy

10. A Solemn Vow of Self-Celibacy tells our second mind what to think about our first mind. It provides it with the blueprint to the follow.

11. If we don't tell our second mind what to think about, using our divine mind, the world will tell it what to think.

12. Whatever our second mind thinks, our Soul will experience.

IT'S ALL ABOUT EGO

I realize that for most people the Ego is defined as arrogant, conceited, big-headed, obnoxious or narcissistic. No one has ever opened your eyes to the reality that Ego is also something you have when you're sad, depressed, lonely, have low self-esteem or self-doubt. Both sides of that Ego coin are the results of our Ego being possessed by someone else.

Neither side captures what Ego actually is, so let's delve into the subject. Let's examine what Carl Jung, noted psychologist, thought about the Ego.

I believe Carl Jung said it best when he said this: *"The world will ask you who you are, and if you say you don't know, then the world will tell you who you are. Who the world tells you that you are becomes your Ego"?* That is the traditional way we developed our Ego. The world tells us who we are before we tell the world who we are and so, the world takes possession of our second mind by telling it who to be.

Based upon Carl Jung's insight, Ego is who we become as a result of comparing ourselves to others, seeking to please them, trying to impress them, proving something to them and secretly competing against them. In other words, our Ego is the person we're trying to be for someone else and not ourselves.

We don't come into this world with an Ego. We develop one after we're born. In some cases, our second mind starts to develop while we're in our mother's stomach. Before the development of our Ego, we only have a divine mind. It is for this reason children tend to be so innocent and pure in their intentions. They're not broadcasting any mixed messages.

Children go all out for what they desire. They pursue what they want with total commitment and passion, that is, until they're second mind develops and is taken possession of by the world. When I say the world, I'm referring to parents, siblings, family members, organized religion, peers, schoolteachers, media, public figures and the list goes on. Everyone starts to weigh in telling our Ego what to think about who we are. Everyone is telling us who to be, and the identity assigned to us that makes the biggest impression on our young Ego becomes the thing that possesses us. When translated that means, that particular identity captures the interest of our Ego. Our Ego then starts to grow into something that someone else told it to be, or not to be, because we hadn't told our Ego who to be yet. In a few minutes, I'm going to explain why.

Once this occurs our second mind starts to move in a different direction than our first mind. Our communication slowly becomes filled with mixed messages. It's because our Ego has a Worldly-focus rather than a Soul-focus.

This is when children start to behave like adults. Now, instead of going all out for what we want we become passive like sheep. We sit on the fence. We don't go all out anymore for anything we desire unless, of course, it's a life or death matter. Take for example, when the doctor says we have to change our eating habits or we're going to die. Or when we lose someone close to us and we didn't get a chance to tell them how we felt about them before they passed. It's only after we've been threatened with death, do we wake up for a few moments to live. Unfortunately, it's not long before, we're right back to sleep.

The reason we end up going back to sleep is because we never took possession of our mind. The world is still telling us who to be. We have yet to tell the world who we are.

That's what taking a Solemn Vow of Self-Celibacy does. It broadcasts one clear message to the universe and everyone we meet. It says, "My happiness is worth it. I'm all in it for me." That's what Self-Celibacy means: I AM ALL IN IT FOR ME. I'm one hundred percent on my own side. No longer am I screwing myself.

Adults pretend like they don't care, if they get what they want or not. It's the foreplay we engage in before we screw ourselves completely. This is our way of trying to mitigate the pain and disappointment we've already imagined ourselves experiencing, because our second mind is not in harmony with our first.

We all have an Ego and there are two fundamental ways in which our Ego can develop. We can either develop a Worldly-Focused Ego or a Soul-Focused Ego. The average person you meet has a Worldly-Focused Ego. Here's why. Remember, what Carl Jung said? *"The world will ask you who you are, and if you say you don't know, then the world will tell you who you are."* Whomever tells you who you are first determines what your Ego is going to focus on - Soul or everyone else.

In the story, Jessica demonstrated that her Ego was more focused on pleasing other people than pleasing herself. So did Trina. Likewise, my Ego focused on what the world says is possible rather than what my divine mind said was a possibility. When I kept trying to screw myself and my family out of the home of our dreams it was because I believed the world more than I believed God. What does that mean? It means I was sitting on the fence, afraid to go all in for my desires. I wasn't practicing Self-Celibacy. I had more trust in my past disappointments than I did in my joy and excitement about the possibility.

When our Ego is Soul-Focused it becomes a reflection of our divine mind. We are empowered with the ability to walk on water, feed the multitudes and even turn water into wine. All the problems in our lives are the result of our Ego being more focused on pleasing the world than fulfilling the mandate written into our Soul.

For Trina, it was the epic courage she demonstrated to stand in solidarity with her own truth that empowered her to experience the redemptive power that comes from turning her Ego back to Soul. In that moment, she received the blessing. When she turned her Ego back to Soul she stepped back into her authentic self. Her Ego became the real Trina and not that version of herself that had been performing and putting on airs to impress other people.

SOUL-FOCUSED OR WORLDY-FOCUSED

Hopefully, you're at least beginning to wonder where you are in all of this. I mean, is your Ego Soul-Focused or Worldly-Focused? Better yet, who are you trying to please?

For the entire first half of my life my Ego was Worldly-Focused. I had moments of being Soul-Focused, but for the most part I was consistently focused on becoming something for other people. I believed I wasn't good enough or intelligent enough. And, so, I was constantly motivated to prove people wrong. My life was driven by conflict and my communication was riddled with mixed messages. I was unknowingly living a reactionary life. The world was setting my agenda for me and I didn't know it. No place I landed fulfilled me. Nothing I accomplished during that time made me happy.

Our attempt to become what someone else wants us to be instead of working to be, and express, more of who we already are reveals that our Ego is Worldly-Focused. When we're Worldly-Focused it's reflected in our psychology. The way we think testifies to the fact that we believe the power of life is not within ourselves. It's outside. Okay, I want you to look for your mind in my description of the worldly train of thought. See if you can see evidence of the way you think.

Of The World Train Of Thought

1. When what we believe other people are thinking about us becomes more important to us than what we're thinking about ourselves, it causes…

2. How we look to become more important to us than how we feel. When this happens, it makes…

3. Being right more important to us than getting what we want. This causes us to…

4. Treat what's not working as more important than what is working. When this happens…

5. Avoiding responsibility becomes more rewarding to us than accepting it.

Did you see yourself? Be honest! Track the flow of your time, energy and attention. Wherever you find yourself depositing the bulk of it is where your primary focus lies.

When we're Soul-Focused our psychology testifies to the fact that we believe the power of life is within ourselves and not without. See if you find yourself in this Soul-Focused train of thought.

Soul-Focused Train Of Thought

1. When what we're thinking about ourselves is more important to us than what anyone else is thinking about us.

2. How we feel becomes more important to us than how we look.

3. Now that how we feel is more important to us than how we look, what we want takes precedence over being right.

4. Since what we want is more important than being right pointing out what's working is more important than pointing out what's not.

5. Finally, because we're focused on what's working, accepting responsibility becomes more rewarding than avoiding it.

Which train of thought resonates most with your present condition? If you saw more of yourself in the Soul-Focused train of thought, then that means you've developed some habits that keep you focused on yourself. As a result, you can feel yourself gaining a greater sense of your own power more and more every day.

On the other hand, if you saw more of yourself in the other train of thought then that means you've developed habits that keep you looking outside yourself. It keeps you believing that either there's something missing from you or there's something wrong with you. As a result, you feel more like a victim every day. That means you keep seeing and believing that no matter what you do, you're still not going to be good enough.

The 5 Habit Of Looking Outside Yourself

You have a habit of:

1. Comparing yourself to other people.

2. Trying to please other people.

3. Seeking to impress other people.

4. Wanting to prove yourself to other people

5. Competing with other people

If you answered, "Yes" to any one of the five habits, then your Ego is definitely of the world. Why only one?

It's because they're all connected. If you practice one, you'll unconsciously practice all the others. They're all different manifestations of our Ego's attempt to impress other people rather than please its own Soul.

The 5 Habits Of Looking Inside Yourself

You have a habit of:

1. Appreciating your uniqueness

2. Caring for others without stipulations

3. Impressing yourself

4. Accepting who you are

5. Cooperating with who you are

If you answered, "Yes" to all five questions then you're Ego is Soul-Focused.

For years, my focus was more worldly than divine, and I didn't even know it. Trying to live up to someone else's expectations of me was so normal that I never questioned it. Even though having a Worldly-Focused Ego keeps us believing that we're not good enough, we still go with it. It's because we wholeheartedly believe that's all there is. We don't know there's an alternative. Besides, it's difficult to see the negative impact something is having on you in a society when everyone else is also caught up in the same trick bag.

AN EGO THAT MIRRORS YOUR SOUL

Psychologists contend that we can't live in this world without developing an Ego. What they're saying is, you can't live in this world without feeling compelled to try to become something for someone else. And sometimes, people see greatness in you before you see it in yourself so, it can be positive. However, when you find yourself driven to live up to someone else's expectations you're going to find happiness escaping you. You'll want to become something for your parents, peers, siblings or schoolteachers, etc. However, who they want you to be isn't necessarily in alignment with who you already are. Who you already are is who God, the Perfect Good, created you to be.

Please get this into your thinking. You didn't come into the world to be become something different from who you already are. The notion that you can be whatever you want to be is a distraction from the truth. You are already who you came into the world to be. Your power is in accepting it. The universe asked you to come into this world as a prescription for solving a particular problem that only you have the vision to solve in your own unique way. You are here to do both God and yourself a favor. It is for this reason that when you fail to accurately represent your truth you feel like an absolute failure. It's because on some level you know that's your primary responsibility, to accurately represent your own truth to the world. Every time you alter it you screw yourself out of the vision you came into the world to offer.

I've thought about what psychologists generally say about what the Ego is for a while now, and I've concluded that psychologists are correct. You can't live in this world (the Matrix) without developing an Ego. You need an earthly identity. Here's the thing, though. Who says your Ego has to be a false character? There is no rule anywhere that says your Ego cannot be a perfect copy of the real you. In other words, if we have to have one, then why not make our Ego in the image and likeness of our authentic self. No more pretending to be something we're not to fit into someone square peg. Let's take possession of our Ego and then direct it to the end of our own choosing. Let that new objective mirror the wishes of our Soul. When your Ego becomes a mirror to your Soul, you bring your whole self to every moment in life.

Taking possession of your mind is another way of saying, you become the person who tells your Ego who to be. The person who defines themselves for themselves takes full possession of their mind.

POSSESSION IS 9/10 OF THE LAW

According to the nine original laws defining property, possession is 9/10 of the law. It's an old expression that means ownership is easier to maintain if one has possession of something and is challenging to enforce if one does not. If someone else has it in their possession, whatever sort of property it may be, then it's difficult to use it for your benefit.

Now, just for a second, imagine that the property I'm referring to is not a material thing. It's your mind, the most valuable property you have that is either in your possession or not. It's your meaning-making machine, your Soul's communicator with the outside world. It's prime spiritual real estate. The quality of life you live is determined by the meaning you make through this machine. Your mind, Ego, is a spiritual mechanism. It's meant to be your Soul's helpmeet. However, at present, the way the world is constructed tells us who we are before we do. The reason this is so is because we experience a little thing called, Spiritual Amnesia.

We experience pain in association with the development of our human bodies in a tiny, dark and tight space, called our mother's womb. We erase the memory of our formation, so that we won't be traumatized by the pain later. The side effect of Spiritual

Amnesia is that it takes us a while to remember who we actually are and why we're here. It takes some people longer than others. It all depends on the conscious level of our parents and the environment they constructed around you.

In most cases, before you can tell your Ego who you are, and thus how to be, the world has already impressed upon your Ego its own definition of you. Until you define who you are for yourself your Ego will remain a prisoner and servant of the world. This is why taking possession of your mind is such a critical part of this process.

That said, pay close attention to what Napoleon Hill revealed in his bestselling book, "Think and Grow Rich." Napoleon Hill's mentor was Andrew Carnegie. At the time, Mr. Carnegie was probably the third richest man in America. Mr. Carnegie told Mr. Hill that the first step to growing rich will require him to take full possession of his mind and then direct it to an end of his own choosing. He would go on to tell him that no one can think and grow rich unless they have full possession of their mind and can direct it to an end of his or her own choosing.

When I first read that statement, I was immediately led to wonder why would he make such an assertion? I believe Mr. Carnegie was revealing a reality most people would find difficult to believe and accept. That is, we don't already have possession of our mind. This is something we all must do for ourselves. We must take total possession of our second mind and then tell it who to be; tell it to be who we already are. Command the genie in the lamp to grant the wishes of our authentic self.

Here's how you will know that you have taken full possession of your mind. I think of what I'm about to share with you as goals or markers to be reached. I call them the Five Principles of Power. I refer to them as such because once you've achieved each goal you will have turned on your power. Each principle seeks to answer one simple question that aligns with that principle.

The Five Principles Of Power

The Principle of:

1. **Reliability:** The goal is to trust yourself completely.
   Can I rely on myself?

2. **Synchronicity:** the goal is for your thoughts to be in sync with who you already are.
   Am I in harmony with myself?

3. **Natural Expression:** the goal is to discover how to put your genius to work for you.
   Do I see the genius in my own genius?

4. **Direction:** the goal is for you to sustain your authenticity from one relationship to another.
   Can I trust my own directions?

5. **Security:** the goal is to be able to share the spotlight with others without causing conflict.
   Do I feel secure about who I am?

Your inability to place a check mark next to any one of these five principles means you still don't have full possession of your mind.

Before I reveal how you're going to take back total charge of your mind I want you to understand how society gained possession of it in the first place. Let me make something clear first. It doesn't matter what your race is because race in America is used to define all of us. Much like the story of Adam, who was given the authority to name things in the garden of paradise. Whiteness named and defined us.

In 1691 in the Colony of Virginia the legal concept of White was invented and became a legal binding law.

Before then there was no such thing as white people. They identified themselves by their nationality, ethnic origins or their religion. The invention of the concept of white, would usher in the age of Whiteness. In other words, being white would become synonymous with having legitimate access to the systems and institutions sanctioned by the government, power. It would be determined by law that no person with any Indian, Mulatto or African blood whatsoever could become white. White would later become the only group eligible to become naturalized citizens of America. The status of White would become an exclusive membership club for Europeans who before this time were not identified as white. There are all sorts of books out there documenting when the Italians, Germens, Irish and Jews became white. If you don't know anything about this, I suggest you take a few minutes to look it up.

The Age of Whiteness would mark the beginning of our racial identities. Soon, we were all assigned a racial category. It is our real political position in society. Once we were assigned a race, we were then systematically educated about what our particular racial identity meant. By the time we turned seven years old, we knew exactly what our racial place was is society. We almost never questioned it. It would literally take centuries before the spell that whiteness weaved over our consciousness would start to unravel.

It took over four hundred years to possess the minds of the Original people, currently referred to as Black people. However, it didn't take the forces that be too long to take possession of the mind of Europeans. It didn't take long because the forces that be gave them something to lose. It gave them the status of white to lose. The same thing would play out with other ethnic groups and people of color. They would be given a chance to play the game of white until it no longer served the will of those who invented it.

There is only one way for someone else to gain possession of another's mind, and that's to put their mind under a spell.

HYPNOTIZE YOUR EGO

Listen to my voice. Concentrate on it. Imagine that I'm right there with you. That's it! Relax! Breath in deeply and each time you do, I want you to picture a waterfall surrounded by a picturesque background. They're butterflies flying around, birds are chirping and there's a cool breezing blowing gently. Feel it. Relax. Give into the relaxation.

In this place there is nothing that you want that you cannot have. You simply speak and it appears like magic. You're in your own Garden of Eden.

There you go, just breathe. Now, your eyes are getting heavier and heavier. You are getting sleepier and sleepier. Now, I'm going to count to ten and when I get to ten, you're going to be all the way asleep.

Okay, you get the picture. I was working to put you in the mindset of someone who is in the process of being hypnotized. The thing about being hypnotized for real is that once you're under, I mean really under you have no real idea that you're under. The voice of the hypnotist can plant suggestions into your subconscious that may cause you to do things of which you're totally unaware.

What if I were to tell you that we've all been hypnotized. We were put under a spell by the use of the same dark magic as Adam and Eve that comes from rejection.

We've all been led to believe that we're not good enough for whatever reason. For some of us it's because of the color of our skin, for others it's gender, sexual orientation or economic status. It's all lies, tricks to make our mind susceptible to wanting to prove our value to the world. It is for this reason that the single greatest threat to an Ego that's of the world is rejection. It's because rejection acts as kryptonite.

It weakens your mind. In other words, the world doesn't tell you that you're complete just as you are. It does the exact opposite. Everywhere you go in society someone is telling you that there's something wrong with you or there's something missing. Even those places that claim to love you just as you are subtly tell you the same thing. You need to change who you are. That's code for you need to cheat on yourself by trying to be what someone else wants you to be. They too are saying how incomplete you are.

The world follows the same blueprint laid out by the serpent in the Garden of Eden. The serpent lied to Adam and Eve and they fell for it. Why? It was because they had never come into contact with a lie ever before in their lives. As I mentioned earlier in the book, they had no way of knowing that they were being lied to.

The serpent tricked them into believing that they weren't good enough, they weren't like God. The thing is the scriptures clearly state that God created them in his own image and likeness. In other words, they were already like God. When the serpent told them that they were not like God it captured their imaginations, in a negative way. It was this lie that allowed the serpent to possess their minds.

There is a psychology to rejection, and I want you to think about it. What is it that gives rejection its sting? It's the desire for acceptance. In fact, the more we desire to be accepted by someone the more we open ourselves up to the possibility of being turned down. However, if our mind is Soul-Focused, rejection is simply looked upon as redirection. But when our second mind is *of the world* rejection can act like dark magic.

Consider what happens in a relationship. One person turns down the advancements of the other. Instead of the rejected person using the rejection as an act of redirection, they become committed to proving to the other person just how worthy they are. In other words, they want the person who rejected them more than they've ever wanted anyone else. From that moment, until they've regained possession of their mind, they will literally go through hell to prove to the other person that they deserve to be accepted by them. Secretly, they will work like hell to make themselves acceptable to the other person.

Without realizing it, their dysfunction will cause them to transfer their power over to the person who has rejected them. In most cases, the person doing the rejecting has no idea this is happening. In other words, they weren't consciously attempting to get the other person to transfer their mind power over to them. In most cases, that is. However, there are rare cases when the person or persons doing the rejecting are well aware of the negative influence rejection has on the mind of the other person. In this case, they intentionally apply rejection as a strategy of spiritual warfare. It acts like a type of dark magic, casting a spell of manipulation over their second mind.

ADAM'S FIRST JOB

If someone else tells you who you are and you buy into it, one way or another, they become the appraiser of your value. You look to them to see if you're doing it right or if you passed the test they've laid before you. Nothing is more dangerous to Ego than rejection.

Have you ever read the book of Genesis in the King James version of the bible? You discover that the first job God gave to Adam was to name every creature in the garden. The power to name something is the power to define what something is or can be. Adam was given this job because he who names a thing determines the circumference and diameter in which that thing can grow into.

The mind works in such a way that whoever we believe we are, our mind will grow into it. That works in the positive and negative. It's a huge power. Think of the mind, as if it were water and the name, definition or identity you prescribe to someone or something as the container that will hold the water. Water once poured into the container will take on its shape. In other words, once your mind starts to focus on that definition, it will take on the ascribed characteristics. This is what is meant by, "As a man thinketh, so is he." It doesn't mean that literally. However, what it's pointing us to is what happens to the mind when it seeks to live up to another's definition of us. It is for this reason rejection is so dangerous.

Now, that doesn't mean that's all the water (mind) is. It means that's what the mind will become until you transmute it into another definition. The real power is in knowing that you are neither the container nor the water. You are the creator of both, the mind and the identity. That's when the real power comes online.

Why did I say all of that? It's because when you don't have full possession of your mind you almost can't help but to believe that you are either the container or you're the water. Thinking either way is problematic because you lose focus on the center.

AT THE CENTER

At the center of you, is the real you, a living being, full of God consciousness. The more aware you become of your God consciousness the bigger you get, meaning the more influence you have in the world. Think of your core as if it were home plate like in the game of baseball, the goal is getting back to Homeplate. Authenticity is the measure. We never fuck ourselves when we're expressing our authentic selves.

There, at your core you will find your authentic voice. It's your signature vibration. Think of it as a unique frequency that acts much like the password or pin number you enter in order to gain access to your bank account. When you speak from your authentic voice all sorts of spiritual doors are opened up to you, both inside yourself and out in the universe. There are doors of consciousness you need to open up in yourself to realize your full growth potential.

Please do not take this lightly nor look upon it as some form of mumbo jumbo. The universe without is the universe that's unfolding from within. The only thing that's stopping you from realizing the fullness of this reality is the fact that you choose to believe that the universe without is coming from somewhere other than within yourself. That, my friend, is an illusion. All things without come from within. This is the nature of life itself. The principle of the seed teaches us this. Everything comes from within. That said, you have to change your point of focus.

Growth is the one and only Will of God, the Perfect Good of all life that exists. That simply means, God wants us all to grow into our full potential expression. Every law in the universe is working to support that one endeavor, growth. Our power comes from growing and when we don't grow, we lack power. No human being does well without power. Power is our very nature because growth is our most natural assignment. Growth is the Will of God.

That being true, it's not that we don't have all the power we need to do whatever we desire to do, right now. It's that we don't have access to that power even though it's right at our fingertips. In other words, we're thinking and doing things that are interfering with our growth. You know what it is; we're screwing ourselves. We're worshiping at the altar of ignorance, out of fear of the responsibility that comes with acknowledging the fullness of our own truth.

You see as long as we continue to believe that life comes from without, then we'll never develop the consciousness that comes with believing the truth. All life comes from within. That is the nature of God, growth. No strategy has proven to be more effective at solving problems than simply outgrowing them.

Here is the only reason why we don't have access to our power. It's because we keep attempting to log into our account with the wrong pin number. Nothing in the universe can respond to someone that doesn't exist. Your pretend self does not exist. Who you're trying to be for other people is your make-believe self. There is no way to authenticate the person you're pretending to be. As long as we keep showing up as an imposter, we'll continue to be unable to get into our spiritual accounts. It is for this reason that each time you show up inauthentic you screw yourself. No one who screws themselves ever grows.

That said, for centuries now, we have failed to accurately represent our truth. At some point we did, as a strategy for survival. In other words, we knew we were pretending to fool our oppressors. However, what we didn't realize is that there are side effects to pretending. Some of the side effects of pretending include, disillusionment, confusion, and the inability to distinguish your performative expression from your natural expression. The likelihood of this occurring is extremely high when you consider the fact that we live in a world that rewards us for our performative expression. What we don't realize is that, our performative expression suppresses our creative genius. In other words, the more we play make-believe, the less innovative and creative we become. Performative expression dumbs down our natural intelligence, lessening our growth potential.

The thing is, the universe is holding you directly responsible for growing. There is only one way for a Being in a human body to grow and that's by accurately representing their own truth. You must take a Solemn Vow of Self-Celibacy.

Just so we're clear, taking a Solemn Vow of Self-Celibacy means you're making a commitment to going all in for yourself. You are ready to broadcast to the world that you're standing in solidarity with yourself. You're not screwing yourself anymore.

Before you take the vow, I'd like for you to read this:

Choice is a word that empowers us to cast a spell on ourselves and we must own the power to choose lest we forfeit our ability to use our magic on ourselves.

Repeat after me:

I am where I am, not because I have to be.

I am where I am because I choose to be, whether I'm conscious of it or not.

My ignorance of the Law of Choice does not take me off the hook for being responsible for what I have manifested in the world through it.

My choice is my magic wand.

My choice is what's delivered me to this moment and only my choice can deliver me to someplace else. When I am ready, I will hoist myself up into a new vibrational frequency and everything in my life will change in a twinkling of an eye.

Before I make my next decision, I need to think about what my last decision taught me. So that the choice I make now takes me somewhere I've never been before that I want to be. Too many of my past choices have only managed to deliver me to precisely where I've already been.

My choice is like the steering wheel in my car; or the coordinates I enter into the computer that guides the rocket to where I want it to land.

I am the navigator. No one can drive me to where I want to be but me and I accept full responsibility for my power to do so.

Today I choose, and I do so, wisely, knowing full well I am a magician with the power to work magic in my own life!

SIGNS AND SIGNALS

Here's what I've been telling you. Your life works in tandem with your communication. Whatever is unfolding in your life, the current consistent conditions are all reflections of the messages you keep conveying to others and yourself through your communication. Your life, your relationship patterns and your experiences are all saying something about the messages you've been giving off to the universe. The only way to fix this communication problem is to take full possession of your mind and then direct it to an end of your own choosing. The beautiful thing is, there's only one thing you have to do to achieve this and that's take a Solemn Vow of Self-Celibacy. Make a commitment to yourself and your Higher Power to never fuck yourself again.

Your reoccurring unhappiness, depression, regrets, resentments, disappointments and upsets are all signals. Much like the warning lights that pop up on the dashboard of your car, they are trying to tell you something. They're not trying to hurt you. Neither are they working against you. In fact, they may be your hardest working angels. They're trying to get you to check underneath the hood of your communication. Check out what's coming from out of your mouth. Without you knowing it, every time you open your mouth, you are speaking your reality into existence.

Those signals aren't trying to tell you that you need to change who you are. In fact, in a big way, they're trying to tell you that you need to maturely express more of who you are. Your problem is not in who you are, it's in the messages you keep broadcasting. Sure, you're saying the right things on your knees in prayer, but you're not saying the right things on the street, on the phone and on social media. Remember what I revealed in the beginning of the book. There is no separate pot of communication. All your messaging melts into one theme and when those messages are conflicting you end up manifesting more of what you already have. In fact, that's proof that you're screwing yourself; you keep manifesting more of what you don't want.

In other words, your yes's aren't yes's and your no's aren't no's. It's a mixed message and in something as seemingly harmless as this, you are unknowingly screwing yourself out of a whole lot of blessings. In a manner of speaking, you're constantly trying to be two places at one time, which means you're not being fully present anywhere. That's the type of effort you've been investing into your life, half in, half out. What do you believe that will manifest?

All throughout my book I've been repeating one major theme, and that is this. Your mixed messaging is screwing you out of your blessings. Right now, you may be looking at your current situation, and thinking to yourself. "I've been in this condition for a long time now. There's nothing I can do to change it." Well, that's not at all true. The first and most powerful thing you can do to totally transform your unwanted circumstances is to start broadcasting one message. Your life should have one theme, and the people around you should know what that theme is.

You start to broadcast one message when you lean all the way into what your Soul desires. When you take your Ego back and then focus it on the Soul everything changes. I'm talking about, going all out for what makes you happy. Giving a one hundred percent effort to yourself. I'm talking about no longer holding back, loving with every fiber of your being. Giving yourself the chance to feel what it feels like to be totally committed to yourself. That's what your life and your communication has been missing, a Solemn Vow of Self-Celibacy.

Consider the fact that you are yet to consistently give yourself all that you got. You keep waiting for someone else to come along and do it for you. Suppose, that job can only be done by you? What if your authentic self is the one you've been waiting to show up and sweep you off your feet? I'm not talking being authentic every now and then. I'm talking about a total commitment to your Higher Power to practice Self-Celibacy everyday of your life.

Just for a moment, imagine how different your life is going to be when you say what you mean, and you mean what you say, daily. See yourself no longer comprising your integrity for anyone. That includes, your spouse, parents, siblings or children. You're standing on your square. You're demonstrating what it looks, sounds, feels and tastes like to be one hundred percent on your own side. Demonstrating this means you totally trust yourself and because you do, you've uncovered the secret to taking advantage of your own brilliance. Now you're able to sustain your authenticity from one relationship to another. That means you're no longer altering yourself for anyone.

Wow! You've made some powerful spiritual adjustments to your communication and because you have you can share the spotlight with others without feeling insecure and causing conflict. That means whatever you create will be solid and sound because you didn't sow any mixed messages into it.

Now, we've come to that point on the journey where it's time for you take the Solemn Vow of Self-Celibacy. I promise, if you take this vow no part of your life will remain the same. Your commitment to practice Self-Celibacy on a daily basis, will at first require an act of courage, but soon it will become the most powerful habit in your life. To be committed to being all in for yourself is not a small thing. The unwanted results you've experienced in your life are all the products of you screwing yourself. You've been lukewarm about a lot of things. It ends today. Today, you tell the world who you are and take back full possession of your mind so you can direct it to the end of your own choosing.

Remember, it's communication that makes the world, go around. Don't you ever forget that. It means, communication is the vehicle that takes you to where you want to go. And the only reason why anyone repeatedly doesn't make it to where they want to go is either because they don't know where they want to go or they're giving off mixed messages. Your communication can only take you to where your clarity is and that is what taking a Solemn Vow of Self-Celibacy will bring to your communication; a commitment to clarity.

THE VOW

On this date, 07/4/2020 I, Berwick Mahdi Davenport, being of sound mind and body make the following confession. Today, I confess my deepest, darkest secret. I am guilty of committing the most perverted spiritual act one can commit. I confess to fucking myself and I've been doing it for a very long time. I am also guilty of blaming others for screwing me over when it was me the entire time. Even when people tried to stop me from fucking myself, I continued. There was no place that was sacred. I screwed myself anywhere and everywhere; at home, work, church, in front of audiences and out in society.

In the past I have failed to demonstrate what it looks, sounds, feels and tastes like to be one hundred percent on my own side every day and I ask myself for forgiveness.

On this day, I take a Solemn Vow of Self-Celibacy and promise to never fuck myself again, under the penalty of universal law. That means, that if I forsake my oath, I understand that the law of reciprocity will be rendered in full effect. There will be no grace to escape what fucking myself brings into my life.

From this day forth. I promise to stand in solidarity with myself, no matter what, as I know that in doing so, the universe has my back. I commit myself to being <u>all in for me</u>. I'm <u>all in for what my Soul desires</u>.

This is my Solemn Vow of Self-Celibacy.

<u>Align your mind with what feels divine, and you will shine!</u> That's the essence of what Berwick Mahdi Davenport, aka "M," CEO of the Soul-Focused Group, has been teaching people for the past thirty years. He is a contemporary spiritual teacher, life performance coach, author, anti-racist educator, and social justice organizer who travels extensively, taking his message throughout the world. He is the father of three beautiful daughters who inspires him daily to contribute to making the world a transformed place of grace, gifts, and favors that benefit us all. No matter what you're seeking to achieve, at the root of it, is a distinct feeling that you want to feel. The right internal atmosphere acts as the spiritual key unlocking the door to your optimal self. Until you feel it, something will feel like it's missing. It's the feeling that you want to perceive within yourself that releases the blessing into your life, fulfillment. Success without fulfillment is, therefore, failure. "M" uses his Soul-

Focused psychology to teach people the purest path to success.

To book M for your conference, zoom presentation and keynote addresses please go to www.soulfocusedgroup.com or email @ Mahdi@soulfocusedgroup.com

Made in the USA
Las Vegas, NV
31 July 2022